CW01151563

Original title:
The Path to Dreamland

Copyright © 2024 Creative Arts Management OÜ
All rights reserved.

Author: Rory Fitzgerald
ISBN HARDBACK: 978-9916-90-794-8
ISBN PAPERBACK: 978-9916-90-795-5

Chasing Ethereal Fantasies

Stars whisper secrets in the night,
Dancing shadows take their flight.
Moonlit paths where wishes gleam,
Chasing dreams in a silver stream.

Heartbeats echo, soft and clear,
Lost in realms where none appear.
With every step, our spirits rise,
Towards the dawn where magic lies.

Voyage into the Dreamscape

Sailing seas of quiet thought,
In the depths, our heart is caught.
Clouds of visions drift and sway,
Guiding us on our secret way.

Each wave a story yet untold,
In this twilight, brave and bold.
Embers flicker, night caress,
In this dream, we find our rest.

Woven Threads of Slumber

In the loom of night, we weave,
Tapestries of dreams we believe.
Colors blend in soft embrace,
While reality finds its place.

Fingers trace the fabric fine,
Stitching memories, yours and mine.
Sleeping whispers fill the air,
As we drift to realms most rare.

Adventures in the Realm of Imagination

Through the gates of thought we roam,
Building castles, calling them home.
Dragons soar and fairies dance,
In this world, we take our chance.

With every turn, a tale unfolds,
Treasures hidden in dreams of gold.
Imagination, wild and free,
Adventures waiting just for me.

Vistas of Enigma

In each shadowed path we tread,
Mysteries unfold, unsaid.
Winds whisper secrets of old,
Through the veil, stories unfold.

Glimmers of truth, elusive and bright,
Dance in the corners, out of sight.
Revelations bloom in the dark,
Casting their spell, igniting a spark.

Windows to the World of Sleep

Curtains drawn, the night awakes,
Into dreams, the spirit breaks.
Hushed lullabies float through the air,
Sailing softly, free from care.

Moonlit journeys, shadows creep,
Guiding us into slumber deep.
Time suspends, as whispers glide,
In this realm, the heart confides.

Whims of Darkness

Night drapes its cloak, heavy and fine,
Unseen forces play, intertwine.
Echoes rise from the depths below,
In shadows lurk, the secrets grow.

A dance of phantoms, sly and bold,
In whispered tales, they lovingly scold.
Enigmas wrapped in a shroud of night,
Guide us along paths of fleeting light.

The Alchemist of Slumber States

Spinning dreams with golden threads,
Crafting realms where silence spreads.
In the stillness, wonders arise,
Alchemy born from midnight skies.

With every sigh, a story we weave,
In twilight's embrace, we dare believe.
Transforming fears into gentle light,
The alchemist dances through the night.

Whispers of Stardust

In the stillness of night,
Stars flicker with delight.
Soft whispers in the dark,
Dance like fireflies' spark.

Galaxies twirl and spin,
Tales of worlds tucked within.
Fragments of light cascade,
Dreams in silence laid.

Cosmic secrets unfold,
Stories waiting to be told.
Each twinkle a soft sigh,
Of the vast, endless sky.

Hearts entwined with the glow,
Lost in the magic flow.
In the gentle night breeze,
Stardust whispers with ease.

Journey through Celestial Meadows

In meadows of the night,
Stars bloom with silver light.
Across the cosmic field,
Wonders are gently revealed.

Planets sway in the dance,
Galaxies in a trance.
Each flower, a spark of dreams,
Flowing in celestial streams.

Soft whispers in the air,
Carried beyond the stare.
Wander through the unknown,
Finding realms to call home.

Every step a new sight,
Guided by starlit light.
In the quiet embrace,
Discovering a new space.

Nighttime Epiphanies

In the hush of the night,
Thoughts take graceful flight.
Ideas bloom like flowers,
Under the moon's soft powers.

Reflections start to weave,
In silence, we believe.
Stars wink in knowing grace,
Illuminating the space.

Epiphanies come clear,
Whispering in the ear.
Each spark ignites the mind,
In the dark, truths are kind.

Awake within dreams' tide,
In the night, we confide.
With each moment that glows,
Wisdom in stillness flows.

Beyond the Horizon of Sleep

In dreams where shadows play,
We drift far away.
Beyond the night's embrace,
To a vast, untouched space.

Softly calling us near,
Visions sharp and clear.
A realm where silence reigns,
And freedom breaks all chains.

Every moment a flight,
Into the starry night.
Seeking what lies ahead,
In whispers, we're gently led.

As dawn begins to creep,
We return from our sleep.
But the dreams forever stay,
Guiding us through the day.

The Roadway of Wishes

Stars flicker above our heads,
Guiding dreams along the way.
Each step whispers secrets,
In the dusk of fading day.

Paths of silver and of gold,
Lead to places unexplored.
With each wish, a story unfolds,
In the night where hearts are stored.

Softly the moonlight gleams,
A tapestry of hopes we weave.
In the silence, we find dreams,
And in believing, we believe.

Trust the road, let it unfold,
The magic lies within the quest.
With each desire, be bold,
For the journey is the best.

Nighttime Nurtured Whims

In the shadows, whispers play,
Gentle sighs come drifting near.
This is where the dreams can sway,
Easing every hidden fear.

Stars awake and softly glow,
Painting stories on the skies.
In this realm, all feelings flow,
Where our wildest wishes rise.

Moonlight cradles thoughts untold,
Hopes and fancies take their flight.
Within our hearts, a warmth we hold,
Nurtured by the breath of night.

Close your eyes, let visions bloom,
In this moment, time stands still.
Amongst the stars, dispel all gloom,
For nighttime nurtures every thrill.

Splendor in the Sleepy Hours

When the world begins to fade,
And shadows stretch, long and deep,
A magic veil begins to cascade,
Wrapping dreams in a tender sweep.

Gentle lullabies fill the air,
In a hush, the heart takes flight.
Magic whispers everywhere,
Creating wonders in the night.

Softly drifting, we explore,
The twilight's mysterious glow.
Each moment invites us to soar,
In the realm of sweet dreams' flow.

With open hearts, we chase the stars,
In sleep's embrace, we find our way.
Splendor blooms, suspending scars,
In the cradle of night's ballet.

Echoing Wishes in the Night

Underneath the sprawling sky,
Whispers linger with the breeze.
In the stillness, wishes fly,
Carried softly through the trees.

Every hope a shining star,
Casting light on dreams at play.
Wanderers, no matter how far,
Find their paths in night's ballet.

Echoes call from deep within,
Stirring echoes of our past.
In the night, a quiet kin,
We find solace, unsurpassed.

Chase the wishes, hold them tight,
For in shadows, visions gleam.
Echoing softly, through the night,
Every heartbeat sounds a dream.

The Limitless Expanses of Night

Underneath the starlit sky,
Dreams unroll like silken threads,
Each twinkle whispers secrets old,
In midnight's arms, our hearts are led.

The moon, a lantern in the dark,
Guides wandering souls through the mist,
With shadows weaving tales untold,
In this vast night, we find our tryst.

Waves of silence gently flow,
As constellations start to play,
Each breath echoes with the stars,
In night's embrace, we drift away.

The limitless stretches far and wide,
With galaxies in a silent dance,
In the night's embrace, we confide,
In dreams, we take our cosmic chance.

Questing through Fantasies

Through swirling mists of dreams we roam,
Chasing echoes in a world unknown,
Each moment spins our tales anew,
In fantasies, we find our home.

The whispers of the wind do call,
Guiding paths to realms so bright,
Where dragons soar and fairies dance,
In vibrant hues, we chase the light.

A tapestry of wishes lies,
Woven with threads of hope and bliss,
Each heartbeat drums the stories on,
In our hearts, impossible dreams persist.

Questing through these winding trails,
We gather treasures, bold and rare,
With every step, a tale unveiled,
In the realm of dreams, we dare.

Fables of the Moonbeam Trail

Along the path of silver light,
Where moonbeams kiss the twilight air,
Legends whisper through the night,
In shadows, tales of love and care.

Each step we take on this bright trail,
Brings memories hushed by time's embrace,
With every turn, a fable sails,
Carried forth by stars in space.

The dance of shadows weaves a spell,
As night descends in soft caress,
With stories told that hearts can tell,
In moonlit dreams, we find our rest.

Fables linger in silent charms,
Alive in the softest of sights,
Through moonbeams, we find our arms,
Wrapped in the magic of the night.

Musings from the Edge of Dreaming

Where shadows weave and whispers call,
The edge of sleep entices all.
Drifting close to visions bright,
In the star's soft, gentle light.

Memories dance like fireflies,
Beneath the vast, unending skies.
Each thought a wave upon the sea,
Carried forth, wild and free.

Moments blend, both real and rare,
Caught in the light, suspended air.
A world where dreams and truths collide,
Awakening hearts, wanting to fly.

So linger here on twilight's seam,
In the delicate thread of a dream.
Let go the day, embrace the night,
And wander through this endless light.

Flickers in the Twilight Hours

Beneath the branches, shadows play,
As dusk transforms the light of day.
Flickers of gold in the faded air,
Hints of magic lingering there.

The breeze carries secrets untold,
In whispers soft, they unfold.
Colors meld in a gentle sigh,
As night unfolds its velvet sky.

Stars emerge with a distant glow,
While the moon casts its silver show.
Each moment a tale, waiting to start,
Stirring the echoes of the heart.

In twilight's grace, let us be still,
Held by the night's enchanting thrill.
For in the quiet, stories ignite,
Flickering dreams in soft twilight.

Journeys Through Enchanted Mists

In mists that cloak the world at dawn,
We wander paths where dreams are drawn.
Treading softly on whispered trails,
Where the heart's longing never fails.

Each step is woven with the past,
In shadows lingering, stories cast.
A realm where time gently sways,
And all is bathed in silken haze.

Mirages beckon with shimmering light,
Guiding us deeper into the night.
We chase the echoes of ancient lore,
Finding wonders lost long before.

So journey forth through the veiled air,
Embrace the magic lingering there.
In enchanted mists, let us trust,
The beauty of dreams, forever a must.

The Allure of the Ethereal Night

Stars call out in a silent choir,
As night drapes all in softest fire.
With every breath, the world stands still,
In the allure of the night's sweet thrill.

Moonbeams dance on the glistening lake,
Awakening dreams that gently break.
A tapestry of shadows and light,
Whispers of wonders hidden from sight.

In this realm where silence sings,
Hope unfurls on delicate wings.
The veil of night, both deep and wide,
Holds secrets that we cannot hide.

So let us wander, lost in flight,
Together in this ethereal night.
For every star that lights our way,
Brings us closer to a brand new day.

Tales from the Dreamer's Den

In the quiet nook where shadows play,
Whispers of moonlight softly sway.
Fragments of visions woven tight,
Bring forth the magic of the night.

Dreams unfurl with a gentle grace,
Dancing in realms we dare to trace.
Stories linger in the air,
Echoes of wishes, soft and rare.

A tapestry spun from hopes and fears,
Laughter and sighs, joy and tears.
In the dreamer's den, all is bright,
Where wishes take flight into the night.

Here in the twilight, time stands still,
Wrapped in a magic that we can't kill.
Come, take a seat, the stories greet,
In the dreamer's den, where hearts beat.

Essence of Midnight Explorations

Beneath the veil of evening's grace,
A path unfolds in shadowed space.
Adventures wait, both far and near,
In the quiet night, we'll lose our fear.

Stars become guides in the velvet sky,
Whispers of secrets, as we fly.
Each step reveals a hidden truth,
Teasing the edges of our youth.

We dance with shadows, we chase the light,
In the embrace of the lonely night.
Hold close the moments, fierce and bold,
In midnight's arms, our tales unfold.

With every heartbeat, the essence swells,
In the exploration, a story dwells.
The world awakens, bright with dreams,
As adventure sings with midnight's themes.

Reflections on the Dreamer's Horizon

Beyond the silence, the horizon gleams,
Where reality mingles with whispered dreams.
A canvas painted in shades of light,
Holds the promise of a brand-new night.

Gaze across the vast expanse,
Where wishes linger, waiting to dance.
Each glimmering star is a tale to tell,
Of hopes and fears, where wishes dwell.

In stillness found within the heart,
Reflections form, waiting to start.
Dreamer's horizon calls us near,
Echoes of laughter, joy, and cheer.

Embrace the magic that freely flows,
In the dreamer's realm, where light bestows.
With open arms and a willing mind,
Discover the dreams we all can find.

Horizons Beneath the Stars

Under the vastness, the cosmos shines,
We share our heartbeats, intertwined.
Every breath whispers tales of old,
Horizons beckon, brave and bold.

Navigating paths where shadows roam,
Together we journey, far from home.
Stars bear witness to the dreams we weave,
In midnight's glow, there's more to believe.

Secrets of stardust spill from our lips,
Guided by visions of celestial trips.
The universe dances, beckoning so,
Rewarding the hearts that dare to glow.

With every glance at the heavens above,
We find our purpose, we find our love.
Horizons beneath the stars unite,
In this cosmic dance, we take flight.

Chasing Clouded Visions

In the haze of morning light,
Dreams entwined in silver mist,
Whispers call from distant heights,
Stories fade, yet still persist.

Windswept echoes softly gleam,
Colors dance in twilight's glow,
Fleeting thoughts begin to stream,
Chasing clouds where shadows flow.

From the depths of hidden fears,
Sights obscure, yet clearly sought,
Hope is woven through the years,
Forgotten paths that time forgot.

As horizons start to blend,
Journey onward, hearts ablaze,
Chasing clouds that never end,
In their dance, we're lost in gaze.

Lullabies of Lost Highways

On forgotten roads we roam,
Where memories weave and wane,
Each curve whispers tales of home,
In the soft embrace of pain.

Stars above sing soothing songs,
Guiding hearts through nights unsure,
Like a river, life flows strong,
Chasing dreams that feel secure.

Time slips by like grains of sand,
Through fingers, silent and sweet,
Echoes haunt this empty land,
Where restless hearts and shadows meet.

In the distance, lanterns gleam,
Illuminating paths once bright,
We drift softly on the stream,
Finding solace in the night.

Footprints in the Velvet Night

Stars sprinkle the darkened sea,
Footprints etched on silken shores,
Waves recede, then beckon free,
In the night, the spirit soars.

Whispers linger with the tide,
Carrying secrets held so tight,
In the dance, where shadows bide,
Footprints fade, lost to the night.

Moonlit paths where dreams collide,
Silent hopes that softly glow,
In the stillness, hearts confide,
As the gentle breezes blow.

Each moment held within the dark,
Echoes of our tender plight,
With every step, we leave a mark,
Footprints intertwined with light.

Escaping into Enchantment

In the heart of twilight's sigh,
Magic lingers on the breeze,
With a glance, enchantments fly,
Whispered notes through ancient trees.

Wonders bloom beneath the stars,
Casting dreams on velvet skies,
Fables woven into bars,
In their glow, our spirits rise.

Chasing shadows, weaving fate,
With each step, the world unfolds,
Time stands still, we hesitate,
Capturing the tales untold.

Lost within this fleeting trance,
In the night, our laughter rings,
Hand in hand, we take our chance,
Escaping where the enchantment sings.

Alignments of the Dream-Sky

Beneath the stars, the cosmos sighs,
Whispers of hope in the endless skies.
Lunar beams dance on silver streams,
In the quiet night, we weave our dreams.

Constellations blink with ancient tales,
Guiding our hearts like gentle sails.
In twilight's glow, the shadows blend,
Where night unfolds, our journeys mend.

Each comet's flight, a fleeting chance,
Enigmas swirl in the midnight dance.
In the vast embrace of astral lore,
We find our paths, forevermore.

The Quadrant of Creative Whispers

In corners dim, ideas ignite,
Whispers of art take glorious flight.
A brushstroke here, a poem there,
In every heart, creativity's flare.

Pencils sketch the dreams we seek,
Fonts of passion in every peak.
Chasing light through vibrant hues,
In this quadrant, we cannot lose.

From clay to canvas, visions bloom,
As silence breaks in a crowded room.
Echoes of genius fill the air,
In the realm of whispers, none compare.

Gardens of the Mind's Eye

In the garden where thoughts entwine,
Flowers of hope in patterns define.
Petals unfurl under a gentle sun,
In silence, creation has just begun.

Paths of wisdom wind through green,
Shadows dance where dreams convene.
Amidst the blossoms, ideas sprout,
In every heartbeat, whispers about.

Gardens flourish, nurtured with care,
Minds awakened, the beauty we share.
In every corner, inspiration lies,
A bounteous land beneath azure skies.

Thoughts Adrift in the Nocturne

Soft echoes fade in the moonlit gloom,
Thoughts adrift in the night's perfume.
Songs of starlight, fragile and sweet,
Memories linger on silvered feet.

Beneath the veil of twilight's grace,
Hopes are cradled in time's embrace.
Waves of silence wash over the land,
In peaceful cadence, we take a stand.

As shadows waltz on the edges of dreams,
The heart whispers softly, or so it seems.
In the nocturne's hold, we come alive,
In drifting thoughts, our spirits thrive.

Threads of Night's Embrace

In shadows deep, where whispers dwell,
The moonlight weaves its silver spell.
Stars twinkle softly, secrets shared,
In night's embrace, the heart is bared.

The misty dance of dreams unfolds,
In shades of twilight, stories told.
Each thread of dark, a path we weave,
In night's embrace, we dare believe.

The silent night, a canvas wide,
Where thoughts take flight, and fears subside.
With every breath, a world we chase,
In gentle night's warm, soft embrace.

As darkness wraps us in its shroud,
We find our peace beneath the cloud.
In threads of night, we come alive,
With every heartbeat, we will thrive.

The Gateway to Enchanted Realms

In whispers soft, the gate appears,
A shimmering light that calms our fears.
With every step, the magic grows,
A world unseen, where wonder flows.

Through ancient woods, where fairies play,
And sunlight dances in bright array.
The trees adorned with secrets old,
In enchanted realms, our hearts unfold.

Each turn reveals a hidden truth,
The spark of dreams, the flame of youth.
With every journey, our spirits soar,
In this fair land, we yearn for more.

The gateway glows with promise bright,
A chance to chase the fleeting light.
Together we'll cross, hand in hand,
To enchanted realms, a wondrous land.

Horizon Beyond Dawn's Embrace

The dawn arrives, a canvas bright,
With hues of hope, it greets the light.
Each ray a promise, freshly spun,
A new adventure just begun.

The horizon whispers tales in gold,
Of journeys vast and dreams untold.
With every breath, the world awakes,
In dawn's embrace, our spirit breaks.

Mountains rise to touch the sky,
With open hearts, we dare to fly.
In radiant glow, our paths align,
Beyond the dawn, the world is mine.

So let us wander, hand in hand,
Across the dunes of golden sand.
The horizon calls, a siren's song,
In dawn's embrace, we all belong.

Flickering Hopes of Starlight

In the quiet of the evening's glow,
Flickering hopes begin to flow.
Stars above, like dreams alight,
Whisper secrets through the night.

Each twinkle tells a tale untold,
Of wishes made and hearts of gold.
In the stillness, we dare to dream,
Flickering hopes in a celestial beam.

The night sky holds our deepest fears,
Yet brings solace through its tears.
With every spark, we find our way,
In starlit paths, we long to stay.

So let us cherish every spark,
As darkness fades and light embarks.
For flickering hopes will always guide,
Our journey through the starlit tide.

A Tapestry of Twilight Tales

In the glow of the fading light,
Whispers dance in the coming night.
Stars awaken with gentle grace,
As shadows weave in their embrace.

Stories linger among the trees,
Carried soft by the evening breeze.
Each leaf tells a tale of old,
Of dreams and secrets, glimmers gold.

The moon listens with silver ears,
To laughter, hopes, and hidden fears.
Twilight's brush paints the scene divine,
A tapestry of night, so fine.

In the heart of dusk, we find our way,
Mapping starlit paths, come what may.
A gathering of souls gently greet,
Under the twilight's rhythmic beat.

Scribes of the Starry Night

Underneath the vast sky's sweep,
The stars, like ink, in silence seep.
Each twinkle writes a line so bold,
A narrative of night, untold.

Scribes dwell in the velvet dark,
Crafting tales with a flickered spark.
Galaxies spin in their glimmering hand,
Casting stories across the land.

Whispers flutter, a cosmic song,
Guiding dreams where they belong.
Constellations breathe, alive and wild,
In the hearts of the restless child.

Night unfolds with pages wide,
In starlit corners where wishes hide.
Scribes pen the magic, pure and bright,
In the heart of the starry night.

Splashes of Dreamy Delights

Colors blend in the evening air,
A canvas rich with dreams laid bare.
Brushstrokes soft as a whisper's sigh,
Dance upon the horizon's eye.

Bubbles burst with laughter's cheer,
Every splash a story near.
In the palette of twilight's grace,
Delights emerge in a sweet embrace.

Dancing shadows play their part,
Echoing the rhythms of the heart.
Starlit visions, dreams take flight,
In the splashes of the fading light.

Let imagination paint the sky,
With vibrant hues that float and fly.
In every droplet, a glimpse of bliss,
In the dreamy world, we won't miss.

Chronicles of the Slumbering Sea

Beneath the waves, where secrets lie,
The sea unfolds, with a gentle sigh.
Each ripple whispers tales of old,
In the chronicles, the ocean told.

Mermaids sing to the moon above,
Crafting dreams with the tides they love.
Shells hold stories, treasures they keep,
Guardians of wonders, deep in sleep.

The horizon fades, where waters blend,
Night's embrace, a calm commend.
In silent depths, the currents weave,
Chronicles of those who believe.

Stars reflect on the tranquil sea,
A mirror for hearts, wild and free.
As slumber blankets the world in peace,
The ocean dreams, and the tales increase.

Chronicles of the Celestial Explorer

In the depths of seas unknown,
Stars whisper secrets softly shown.
A vessel carved from ancient lore,
Navigates the endless shore.

Galaxies spin in silent grace,
Time and space, their warm embrace.
Each comet's tail, a story bold,
In starlit ink, the tales unfold.

Darkness holds a vibrant light,
Twinkling dreams that chase the night.
Through cosmic winds, the explorer flies,
With wonder gleaming in their eyes.

In the silence, wisdom waits,
Beyond the void, open gates.
Chronicles woven on astral streams,
We are but echoes of our dreams.

Journeys in the Nebula of Dreams

Within the mist of twilight hues,
Whispers of a fateful muse.
Stars like petals drift and sway,
In nebulae where shadows play.

Through velvety paths of stardust gold,
Each heartbeat gives the dreamer bold.
Wonders hidden, gently gleam,
Awakening thoughts from the dream.

Beyond the edges of what is known,
Transcendent realms where seeds are sown.
Each flicker tells a tale profound,
In cosmic silence, wisdom found.

The journey swells like ocean tides,
With swirling stars as endless guides.
A tapestry of night unfurls,
In the vastness of dreaming worlds.

Paths Within Celestial Landscapes

Through the void of whispered light,
Celestial paths weave out of sight.
Between the stars, a dance unfolds,
Mapping dreams in hues of gold.

Mysterious shapes in cosmic play,
Guide the wanderers on their way.
Each nebula, a painted scene,
Where fantasies weave and spirits glean.

With every pulse, the universe sighs,
A symphony that never dies.
Footprints on the astral shore,
Tell of journeys, longing for more.

In the tapestry of space and time,
Echoes linger, gentle rhyme.
Paths within the landscape soar,
Leading seekers to distant shores.

Echoes of Somnolent Secrets

In the cradle of a velvet night,
Somnolent thoughts take fragile flight.
Echoes shelter in twilight's arms,
Whispering lost and gentle charms.

Beneath a canopy of dreams,
Sleepy starlight gently beams.
The secret longings of the heart,
In shadowed corners, still play their part.

Memories drift like cherry blossoms,
Floating free, without a cause.
Each petal holds a story told,
Of hopes and fears, and dreams of old.

In silent nights with time suspended,
Secret sighs remain unended.
Echoes throughout the cosmos sing,
Of somnolent whispers that time can bring.

Startled by Moonlight

The silver glows upon the lake,
A sudden chill, a gentle shake.
Whispers of the night unfold,
The stories of the stars retold.

Shadows dance upon the ground,
In quietness, the world surrounds.
Caught in wonder, hearts in flight,
Startled softly by the light.

A fleeting glance, the moment stays,
As night entwines the dusky rays.
Breeze carries secrets, dreams to spin,
In moonlit realms, where thoughts begin.

Through branches swaying, echoes call,
The magic of the night enthralls.
Though lost and found in silver gleam,
We wander forth, embraced in dream.

Dust from a Dreaming Mind

Whispers rise like morning fog,
Thoughts entwined in whispered smog.
Dusty corners softly gleam,
Fleeting moments weave a dream.

Memory's touch, a gentle sigh,
Carried forth as days drift by.
Fragments catching in the light,
Dust from visions takes its flight.

A tapestry of hopes and fears,
Woven through the passing years.
Every thought a grain, it seems,
Dust collected from our dreams.

Silken threads in twilight spun,
Weaving tales 'til day is done.
With every breath, we shape and mold,
The story that our hearts have told.

Gazing into the Dreamwell

In a quiet place, I find my gaze,
Deep within the misty haze.
Reflecting dreams that softly flow,
In the depths of the dreamwell's glow.

Ripples swirl, and thoughts collide,
Beneath the surface, worlds reside.
Each flicker tells a tale untold,
In lucid waters, hearts unfold.

Yearnings whisper, visions dance,
Inviting me to take a chance.
I reach for stars within the depths,
Gazing at what the silence kept.

A journey starts within this space,
As shadows blend with time and place.
Entranced by mysteries so well,
I lose myself in the dreamwell.

Navigating the Mind's Labyrinth

Lost within the maze I roam,
A twisting path that feels like home.
Thoughts like whispers on the breeze,
Winding through like rustling leaves.

Echoes bounce off shadowed walls,
In silence, every answer calls.
With every turn, a choice unfolds,
Secrets kept, and stories told.

Flickers of light guide my way,
In this intricate ballet.
Each corridor, a tale to share,
Navigating with gentle care.

As I wander, fears take flight,
Revealing truths within the night.
In this dance of mind and heart,
I find the paths that set me apart.

Transcendent Journeys of the Mind

In whispers soft, the thoughts take flight,
Where dreams entwine with endless night.
A canvas vast, imagination's brush,
In colors bright, we silence the hush.

Through realms unseen, the visions play,
Guided by stars that light the way.
With every heartbeat, a truth unfolds,
In sacred tales, the heart beholds.

To wander free in mental streams,
Where every shadow births new dreams.
The tapestry of fate we weave,
In journeys deep, we learn to believe.

Awake, we chase the fleeting spark,
Through wisdom's flame, we find the dark.
In silent whispers, secrets bind,
Transcendent paths of the open mind.

Celestial Highways of Wonder

Upon the roads of starlit skies,
Where moonlight dances, gleams and flies.
We traverse lanes of glowing light,
In celestial dreams, we take our flight.

Galaxies spin in a cosmic waltz,
With every heartbeat, wonder exalts.
The universe sings with a gentle grace,
In every corner, a sacred space.

Past comets' tails, we boldly sail,
On cosmic winds, we tell our tale.
Nebulae bloom like flowers bright,
In the embrace of eternal night.

In whispers soft, the heavens call,
As we embark, we fear no fall.
In cosmic realms where dreams collide,
On celestial highways, we abide.

The Gateway of Nighttime Reverie

When shadows drape the world in blue,
A portal opens, revealing clues.
In nighttime's hush, our spirits roam,
Through veils of dreams, we find our home.

The stars align in patterns rare,
Each twinkle whispers of what we dare.
In reverie, our thoughts take flight,
To wander realms beyond our sight.

Each echo of the midnight chime,
Invites the heart to dance with time.
In silence deep, we paint the night,
With tales of love, of loss, of light.

Embrace the stillness, let thoughts flow,
In nighttime's arms, our spirits grow.
Through veils unseen, we find our way,
At the gateway where dreams hold sway.

Secrets of the Stardust Trail

Upon the trail where stardust glows,
Whispers of ancient secrets flow.
Each twinkle tells a story deep,
Of cosmic journeys, dreams we keep.

With every step, the past ignites,
A tapestry of woven nights.
In celestial dust, we find our place,
Among the echoes of time and space.

Beneath the moon's soft, silver beam,
We chase the shadows of a dream.
In every spark, a universe lies,
Guiding us through the midnight skies.

Tread softly on the stellar way,
For in the dark, the secrets play.
Embrace the wonder, let heart unveil,
The hidden truths of the stardust trail.

Upon the Wings of Reverie

Dreams take flight on soft, white clouds,
Whispers of wishes wrapped in shrouds.
Through fields of stars, we softly glide,
In the cradle of night, our thoughts abide.

Fleeting visions dance in the dark,
A symphony played by the longing heart.
Each stroke of light, a tale to tell,
In the world of dreams, we know so well.

Time bends and sways, a gentle tease,
Breathing the magic, we find our ease.
In the realm where the shadows sigh,
We live forever, just you and I.

Mysteries of the Dreamscape

In the depths where silence roams,
A tapestry woven with whispered tones.
Mysteries linger like dew on grass,
In the folds of time, as moments pass.

Shadows dance on the edge of thought,
Secrets held in the dreams we sought.
Beneath the stars that brightly gleam,
The mysteries dwell, alive in dreams.

Fleeting phantoms prance and play,
Guiding our dreams, night turns to day.
In the canvas of night, we explore,
Unraveling truths behind every door.

The Cartographer of Fantasies

With ink and quill, he maps the skies,
Charting the path where a dreamer flies.
From realms unknown to shores so bright,
He captures the magic of day and night.

Each line draws forth a tale untold,
Of heroes brave and treasures bold.
In the lands of whims where wishes bloom,
He guides our hearts through the swirling gloom.

With every stroke, a world is born,
Adventurous souls in twilight's dawn.
The cartographer's gift, a woven thread,
Leading us onward, where dreams are fed.

Sojourns in Imaginary Isles

Upon the waves of thought we sail,
To islands bright and wondrous trails.
Each step we take reveals a view,
In lands of fantasy, oh so true.

Palm trees sway in a soft sea breeze,
Carrying laughter, carrying pleas.
Golden sunsets paint the sky,
In this realm where spirits fly.

Here, friendships blossom, wild and rare,
In the heart of dreams, we shed our care.
With every sojourn, we find our light,
In imaginary isles, so pure, so bright.

Paths Made of Light

Along the trail where shadows fade,
A golden hue begins to wade.
Steps softly tread on beams aglow,
In twilight's dance, our spirits flow.

Each moment shines, a fleeting spark,
Illuminating journeys dark.
With every breath, a story spins,
In the warmth where hope begins.

Together we walk, lost and found,
On paths where destiny unbound.
The light we share, a guiding star,
Leading us home, no matter how far.

A chorus lifts, the night ignites,
With whispered dreams and endless sights.
Our hearts in sync, a vibrant tide,
On these paths made of light, we glide.

Echoing Dreams and Silent Whispers

Underneath the moon's soft gaze,
We cast our thoughts in gentle ways.
In shadows dance, the echoes play,
With whispers woven, night and day.

Each dream a tale, a starry thread,
In silent depth, our hopes are fed.
The universe hears each soft plea,
In woven silence, we are free.

Cascading lights on midnight's shore,
Bring forth the dreams we can't ignore.
Through every sigh, our spirits soar,
With silent whispers, we explore.

As dawn approaches, shadows flee,
In echoes strong, we find the key.
With hearts aligned, the mysteries thrust,
Together we walk, in dreams we trust.

Unfolding the Canvas of Night

A tapestry of stars appears,
The night unfolds, erasing fears.
Each twinkling dot, a story spun,
In cosmic depths, the day is done.

The canvas spreads with colors bold,
In dreams and thoughts, new tales unfold.
With brushes dipped in twilight's hue,
We paint a world that's fresh and new.

In stillness wrapped, we find our peace,
As all the busy sounds decrease.
The whispers flow like gentle streams,
In quiet moments, we weave dreams.

With every stroke, a life ignites,
In the vastness of moonlit flights.
Together, we grace this endless night,
Unfolding joy, our hearts unite.

The Alchemy of Dreams

In twilight's grasp, the magic swirls,
Transforming thoughts as the night unfurls.
Each wish, a spark, ignites the air,
In the silence, we breathe and dare.

The alchemy of hearts ignites,
Through whispered hopes and starry nights.
In realms unseen, we shift and roam,
With every pulse, we find our home.

From shadows deep, new visions rise,
In fragments kissed by starlit skies.
The essence of dreams, pure and true,
Transforms our world with every view.

Together we blend, our souls entwined,
In this dance of dreams, we're defined.
With every heartbeat, we weave and scheme,
In the alchemy of dreams, we beam.

Echoes of a Dreaming Heart

In night's embrace, whispers play,
Capturing thoughts that drift away,
A tapestry of hopes unspun,
Where fragile dreams dance with the sun.

Restless beats in silence call,
Casting shadows, soft and small,
Yearning hearts on distant shores,
Find their voice, as darkness soars.

Beneath the stars, a longing sigh,
Echoes of love that never die,
A serenade of faded light,
Guides the soul through endless night.

Memories woven in twilight's grasp,
Holding moments that forever clasp,
A dreaming heart shall never part,
From the echoes that once did start.

Lanterns of the Imagination

Flickering flames in the quiet dark,
Illuminate thoughts with a gentle spark,
Ideas dance like shadows and light,
In the vast corners of dreaming night.

Each lantern glows with a story untold,
Casting warmth on the brave and bold,
Threads of the mind weave wild and free,
In the realm of what could be.

Colors swirl in the misty air,
Painting worlds with vivid flare,
Boundless wonders, so far to roam,
In the heart, they find a home.

With every flicker, inspiration grows,
Unfolding paths as the knowledge flows,
Lanterns aglow, guiding the way,
Through the night into the day.

Shadows of Possible Worlds

Beneath the surface of what is known,
Lies a tapestry of dreams that have grown,
Shadows whisper of paths untraveled,
Making the mind's wild wander unravel.

Each shadow blurred, a tale to weave,
Of choices made and ones to leave,
A realm of wonders beyond the sight,
Where every flicker ignites delight.

In the corners of forgotten space,
Possible worlds take shape and grace,
The heart explores with curious eyes,
As imagination unfurls and flies.

For within each shadow, a glimpse remains,
Of destinies forged in laughter and pains,
Dancing lightly on edges of time,
Crafting the rhythm, a secret rhyme.

Wayfarers in the Land of Nod

Drifting gently on evening's tide,
Wayfarers wander with dreams as a guide,
In the Land of Nod, so soft and still,
Hearts open wide to the night's gentle thrill.

Moonlit pathways lead the way,
To shores where visions freely sway,
Every step whispers tales anew,
In this land for the brave and true.

Nights of wonder, lost in thought,
In slumber's embrace, all battles fought,
With every breath, the dreams unfold,
A tapestry rich, a legacy bold.

Together we roam through realms of sweet grace,
With hope in our hearts, we find our place,
In the warmth of the night, hand in hand,
Wayfarers dream in this enchanted land.

Radiant Horizons of Quiet Wonder

Where the sun greets the dawn softly,
Colors dance in the early light,
Each hue whispers dreams untold,
A promise of a day bright.

Breezes carry the scent of hope,
As petals bloom in the fields wide,
Nature sings its serene refrain,
With beauty, the heart will abide.

Mountains stand with an ageless grace,
Guardians of secrets they hide,
In their shadows, whispers linger,
Of ancient tales, deep and wide.

The horizon calls with a gentle sigh,
Inviting us to explore more,
In quiet wonder, we venture forth,
To discover what life has in store.

Stars that Sing to Sleep

In the blanket of night, they shimmer,
Stars twinkle in a cosmic dance,
Soft melodies drift on the breeze,
Lulling dreams into a trance.

Moonlight bathes the world in silver,
Each beam, a whisper of peace,
As shadows waltz with quiet grace,
Heartaches fade, momentarily cease.

Beneath their watchful, twinkling eyes,
We find solace in dark's embrace,
Their harmonious lullabies hum,
Guiding us to a tranquil place.

So let the stars weave their magic,
As we surrender to the night,
In the arms of sleep, we journey on,
Till dawn breaks with golden light.

Ways to Wonderland

Through enchanted woods, we wander,
Where colors burst in vibrant hues,
Every step, a new discovery,
In realms where magic we choose.

Whispers of fairies fill the air,
Guiding us on paths unseen,
With each twist, the world unfolds,
A tapestry of dreams serene.

Rivers flow with sparkling laughter,
Flowers hum a blissful tune,
The sun smiles down on our journey,
Chasing away the shadows of gloom.

In Wonderland, our hearts take flight,
With friends anew and joy's embrace,
We'll chase the stars and touch the sky,
In this whimsical, timeless space.

Journey Through Slumber

In the realm where dreams take flight,
We sail on clouds of silver gray,
The moon our guide, the stars our friends,
As night gently cradles the day.

Through valleys deep and mountains high,
Whispers of hope round every bend,
Each journey a tale in the making,
As slumber's soft wings descend.

Time loses weight in this stillness,
As we dance on the edge of dreams,
A world where imagination flows,
And nothing is quite as it seems.

With every breath, we drift further,
Into realms where our spirits soar,
In the embrace of the night, we find,
A voyage to cherish and explore.

Moonlit Sojourns

In silver light the paths unfold,
Whispers of secrets, stories untold.
Footsteps soft on ancient stones,
Under the gaze of the moon's bright tones.

Stars twinkle like eyes, bright and clear,
Guiding souls, drawing them near.
Silhouettes dance in the gentle breeze,
Carried away on night's quiet ease.

A river flows, reflecting the skies,
Where dreams, like ships, start to rise.
Each ripple a note in nature's song,
Echoing softly where we belong.

As night weaves its tapestry wide,
We wander freely, hearts as our guide.
The moon, our lantern, lighting the way,
In moonlit sojourns, come what may.

Gardens of Forgotten Wishes

In twilight's embrace, the blooms appear,
Soft petals hide dreams that once were dear.
Each fragrance whispers a past refrain,
Of hopes neglected, lost in the rain.

Among the shadows, memories creep,
As time weaves silence, secrets to keep.
A willow hangs low, its branches weep,
For wishes that slipped, like grains of sleep.

Stars peek through the clouds, shy and bright,
Guarding the garden from the night.
Each blade of grass tells a tale anew,
In the hush of the moon, the hopes accrue.

With gentle hands, we tend and mend,
In gardens guarded, our dreams descend.
For every wish that the heart does cast,
A blossom awaits, bringing forth the past.

Dance of the Dreamweavers

In the quiet of night, they gather near,
Spinning threads of joy, banishing fear.
With laughter like silk and whispers of light,
They weave through the shadows, a wondrous sight.

Fingers entwined, they sway and glide,
Through realms of slumber, with grace they ride.
Each dream a tapestry, colors collide,
Crafting the futures where hopes can abide.

The moon, a spectator, watches with glee,
As they dance through the cosmos, wild and free.
Embracing the magic, the moments unfold,
In rhythm divine, their stories are told.

When dawn kisses night, they fade from view,
Leaving behind a sparkle, a hue.
Yet in our hearts, their footsteps remain,
In the dance of the dreamers, no joy is in vain.

Echoes of a Distant Lullaby

From hills afar, a song drifts low,
A lullaby sweet, in twilight's glow.
It wraps around the weary and worn,
A promise of peace, in silence reborn.

Soft notes rise like mist from the earth,
Stirring the memories, recalling their worth.
Each echo a heartbeat, steady and true,
In the arms of the night, it calls out to you.

The stars blink in rhythm, keeping time,
With hidden wonders wrapped in a rhyme.
As shadows entwine with the dreams we chase,
The lullaby lingers, a tender embrace.

For those who listen, the night holds the key,
To the secrets and wonders of all that could be.
In this melody soft, let your spirit fly free,
With echoes of lullabies, eternally.

Navigating the Dreaming Sea

In a boat of whispers, we sail,
Guided by the moon's soft trail.
Waves of hopes, in silence gleam,
Lost in the heart of a fleeting dream.

Stars above like lanterns bright,
Pointing paths in the tranquil night.
We chase the echoes, we chase the tide,
On a canvas where wishes abide.

The horizon blurs with a brush of fate,
As time sways gently, a lover's gait.
With every stroke, new worlds unfold,
In the depths of the sea, stories told.

Awake to the symphony of the sea,
Where dreams intertwine, wild and free.
Navigating through whispers of time,
In this realm, our souls shall climb.

Visions in the Twilight Fog

In twilight hues, the world awakes,
Wrapped in mist, where silence breaks.
Shapes and shadows dance and swirl,
As we step softly, hearts unfurl.

Glimmers of gold through grayish veils,
Whispering secrets of forgotten trails.
Each breath a story, woven tight,
In the embrace of the coming night.

The fog whispers truths we cannot see,
Dreams unfold in mystery.
In this liminal space, we trust,
Feeling the pulse of the earth's soft lust.

Visions arise, like stars in flight,
Guiding us through the dense twilight.
With every step, we dance and weave,
In the fog's embrace, we dare believe.

Embracing the Moon's Embrace

Under the glow of the silver sphere,
We find solace, we hold dear.
In her embrace, our dreams take flight,
Bathed in her calming, gentle light.

A tapestry of shadows and beams,
We wander through the land of dreams.
Her song caresses the whispered night,
As we drift further into her sight.

With each phase, she whispers fate,
Guiding our hearts, a nurturing mate.
Together we sway, like trees in breeze,
In her soft glow, the world finds ease.

Embraced by the moon, we rise and fall,
In her stillness, we hear her call.
With every heartbeat, we intertwine,
Lost in her glow, forever divine.

Shadows of Slumbering Stars

Beneath the vastness, the stars softly gleam,
In shadows they whisper, sweet secrets of dream.
Each flicker a tale, a memory bright,
Guiding lost souls through the depth of night.

As blankets of twilight wrap the earth tight,
We drift in the arms of the sleeping night.
Stars become lanterns that light up our path,
In the hush of their glow, we escape the math.

In stillness we seek what the night has to show,
The mysteries whispered in the soft starlit glow.
Through echoes of silence, our hearts learn to dance,
In shadows of stars, fate gives us a chance.

The cosmos above hums a lullaby sweet,
As slumbering stars cradle our heartbeat.
Together we wander, in night's warm caress,
In shadows we find our eternal fortress.

The Secret Garden of Sleep

In quiet corners shadows creep,
Where whispers weave and secrets keep.
A world is born in velvet night,
Where dreams take shape in silver light.

Among the blooms where silence reigns,
A gentle breeze through soft remains.
The petals sigh beneath the stars,
Inviting all beyond their bars.

With every breath, the stillness calls,
In this haven, peace gently falls.
The heart, it dances, light and free,
In a garden of serenity.

So close your eyes and drift away,
Let the dreamscape guide your way.
In slumber's arms, we'll find our place,
The secret garden, our embrace.

Maps of Moonlit Fantasies

Beneath the glow of silver beams,
A tapestry of whispered dreams.
Each star a dot upon the way,
Guiding hearts where night holds sway.

In every corner, stories dwell,
Of magic spells, and wishes fell.
With every sigh, the maps unfold,
To fantasies that soon be told.

Adrift in waves of lunar light,
We chase the shadows, hold them tight.
With every step on paths unseen,
Our souls ignite, our hearts convene.

So take my hand, let's wander far,
Through moonlit lands where visions are.
In dreams we'll find what we have sought,
The maps of night, with joy, we're caught.

The Quest for Celestial Bliss

A journey born from hearts that long,
To find the place where we belong.
With stars above to light the way,
We travel forth at break of day.

Through cosmic seas, so vast and wide,
We chase the dreams that universe hides.
Each comet's tail, a path to trace,
In search of love, our sacred space.

With every moment, wonder grows,
In secret realms where starlight flows.
The quest is long, the night is deep,
Yet in our hearts, the promise keeps.

So lift your gaze, embrace the sky,
Our souls entwined, we learn to fly.
In blissful realms where spirits soar,
We'll find the peace we've searched for more.

Sails on a Sea of Dreams

With sails unfurled, we drift away,
On waves of night, in soft array.
The stars above, our compass bright,
As whispers guide us through the night.

Each dream a wave that gently swells,
A melody of secret spells.
The ocean hums a lullaby,
Embracing all who wish to fly.

In every swell, a tale begins,
Of distant shores and whispered sins.
We dance upon this moonlit tide,
With every heartache cast aside.

So let us sail where dreams abound,
In this vast sea, true love is found.
With every breath, we'll chase the gleam,
Forever bound on seas of dream.

Flickering Lanterns in the Mind's Eye

In shadows dance the lights, so bright,
Whispers of dreams take elegant flight.
A flicker here, a glow over there,
Guiding lost souls with tender care.

Memories wrapped in amber hues,
Gentle echoes, vibrant clues.
Each lantern glows, a tale to share,
Illuminating paths with utmost flair.

Through winding thoughts, my senses roam,
Finding solace, a place called home.
Each flickering flame, a beacon true,
In this dark night, I find what's new.

Flickering lanterns stir the night's sky,
Reminding my heart of the reasons why.
With every glow, I touch the past,
In their embrace, my shadows cast.

Celestial Journeys Beyond Time

Stars are maps on the velvet sea,
Charting courses for the wild and free.
In cosmic trails, my spirit glides,
A dance with planets, where wonder resides.

Galaxies whirl in timeless grace,
Chasing echoes of a boundless space.
Each moment stretches like a comet's tail,
On this journey, I cannot fail.

Nebulae whisper secrets so old,
Stories of stardust softly told.
Between the worlds, my heart takes flight,
In celestial dreams that span the night.

Beyond time's grasp, in cosmic streams,
I chase the light, I chase my dreams.
In this vast expanse, I learn to soar,
Celestial journeys forevermore.

Kaleidoscope of Midnight Thoughts

Fragments swirl in a restless mind,
Colors blend, the night unlined.
Thoughts collide, a vivid display,
A tapestry woven from shades of gray.

Shadows flicker like candlelight,
Casting patterns in the cool of night.
Moments shimmer, both near and far,
Painting visions beneath the stars.

In this kaleidoscope, truth unfolds,
Whispers of dreams and tales retold.
Every twist reveals hidden schemes,
A mosaic of hopes, of silent dreams.

From midnight's grasp, my spirit flies,
Through vibrant hues, where the heart lies.
In this space of chaos and calm,
I find my peace, my soothing balm.

Whimsical Wanderings in the Dreaming World

Through fields of whimsy, I take my flight,
Chasing shadows in the pale moonlight.
Butterflies dance on the silk of air,
In this dreaming world, free from care.

Each step unfolds a mystery's tale,
A waltz with wishes, a soft exhale.
Clouds drift lazily, soft as cheek,
In this realm, tranquility speaks.

Stars twinkle playfully in my eyes,
Mirrors of wonder fill the skies.
Every breath, a chance to explore,
In these wanderings, I seek much more.

Whimsical paths lead to distant shores,
Unlocking secrets behind hidden doors.
In a world of dreams, my heart finds grace,
In this timeless dance, my spirit's place.

A Sojourn in Starlit Realms

In twilight's glow, we roam the skies,
With whispered winds and ancient sighs.
Stars above, like lanterns bright,
Guide our souls through endless night.

We dance on dreams, the cosmos wide,
In velvet silence, we confide.
Galaxies spin, our hearts entwined,
In starlit realms, true peace we find.

Each twinkle tells a tale untold,
Of love and courage, hearts so bold.
The universe, our canvas vast,
A journey forged, forever cast.

As dawn draws near, the stars will fade,
Yet in our hearts, their light is laid.
We'll carry forth this cosmic dance,
In every dream, we'll find our chance.

Between Reality and Reverie

In shadows cast, the day will wane,
A thin veneer of joy and pain.
Thoughts drift like clouds across the blue,
Between the real and dreams anew.

The world outside begins to blur,
In silent thoughts, I feel the stir.
A bridge of hope, I dare to cross,
In this sweet space, I feel no loss.

Whispers of dusk, a gentle trace,
In twilight's arms, I find my place.
In fleeting moments, truth will gleam,
As I float in this waking dream.

Each heartbeat sings a secret song,
Where night and day can both belong.
I linger here, where dreams create,
A tender bond between love and fate.

The Harmony of Hidden Dreams

In quiet corners of the mind,
A melody of dreams we find.
Soft echoes dance, like fleeting light,
In whispered hopes that take their flight.

Each secret wish, a gentle tune,
Awakens hearts beneath the moon.
Through tangled thoughts, we search, we seek,
In silent realms, our spirits speak.

The harmony of shadows play,
Where fears dissolve and doubts decay.
In every note, a spark ignites,
Transforming pain to soaring heights.

We weave a symphony divine,
With every heart, our dreams align.
In unity, our truths will stream,
Together we, compose the dream.

Echoes from a Forgotten Realm

In ancient woods where spirits dwell,
The echoes weave a timeless spell.
Whispers call from ages past,
In shadows deep, our dreams are cast.

A crumbling stone, a tale unveiled,
Of lovers lost and ships that sailed.
Their laughter lingers in the air,
A haunting song of love and care.

Beneath the moon, we trace their steps,
In every hush, our souls accept.
The mysteries of yesteryears,
Awake the heart, dissolve the fears.

In twilight's grasp, we find the thread,
Connecting dreams to those once dead.
For time may fade, but love remains,
In echoes soft, their truth retains.

The Dance of Will-o'-Wisps

In twilight's breath, they gently sway,
Flickering lights, they lead astray.
A haunting melody fills the air,
Whispers of magic, a secret to share.

They beckon the lost with shimmering glow,
Ever elusive, they twirl and flow.
Among the shadows, they dance and glide,
In the realms of night, they softly bide.

A flicker here, a shimmer there,
Guiding the dreamers with ethereal flare.
Into the depths, where mysteries gleam,
The will-o'-wisps live in every dream.

So follow their light, but heed their song,
In this enchanted waltz, you can't go wrong.
With each step forward, lose yourself free,
In the dance of wisps, where souls learn to be.

Underneath a Canopy of Wishes

Beneath the stars, where dreams reside,
Wishes float on a silver tide.
Each twinkling light, a hope in flight,
Underneath a canopy, draped in night.

The whispers of longing drift through the trees,
Carried along by the gentle breeze.
Petals of thoughts upon the ground,
In this hidden realm, magic is found.

With every breath, a secret is spoken,
Hearts intertwine, though words remain broken.
In the glow of lanterns, truth softly shimmers,
Underneath wishes, the heart of the dreamer glimmers.

So gather your dreams, release them with care,
And on this night, let your spirit share.
For underneath wishes, where love is made,
Hope dances alive in the softest shade.

Fantasies in the Fog of Night

In the shroud of dusk, where shadows creep,
Fantasies dwell in the silence deep.
Waves of fog, like whispers of lore,
Carry the tales of those gone before.

Figures emerge, then fade away,
Dancing in dreams until break of day.
With each step taken, the veil grows thin,
Revealing the secrets that linger within.

The moon casts a glow on ethereal sights,
Painting the world in magical lights.
In this smoky embrace, truth intertwines,
As fantasies blossom like wild vine.

So wander the mist where the lost reside,
In the fog of night, let your heart be your guide.
For within the hush, treasures unfold,
Fantasies waiting, in courage be bold.

The Call of the Dreamweaver

In the quiet dawn, a whisper calls,
The dreamweaver dances, as twilight falls.
Threads of silver, each one a tale,
Woven with magic, in twilight's veil.

With gentle fingers, she shapes the night,
Crafting illusions, where shadows ignite.
Her loom spins worlds, both bright and dark,
In every heartbeat, a flickering spark.

Listen closely, for time starts to bend,
As reveries swirl, and realities blend.
The call of the dreamweaver weaves through the air,
Guiding the seekers, with love and care.

So take up the thread, let your spirit fly,
In the realm of dreams, where limits defy.
For in her embrace, we find our song,
The call of the dreamweaver, where we belong.

Whispers of Midnight Wanderings

Soft echoes call, the night is deep,
Shadows dance where secrets leap.
Stars above speak in silent tones,
Guiding the heart to unknown homes.

Moonlight weaves a silver thread,
In quiet dreams where few have tread.
Footsteps light on softest ground,
In whispers found, the lost are bound.

Breezes carry stories old,
In every breath, adventures bold.
Through misty paths, the soul will glide,
In whispers soft, true magic hides.

Beyond the Veil of Sleep

In realms where shadows softly sway,
The dreams begin to find their way.
Veils of slumber gently lift,
Revealing all the night's sweet gift.

A tapestry of visions flows,
Where midnight secrets lie in rows.
Timid hearts embrace the night,
While starlit wonders take to flight.

Beyond the veil, a world unfolds,
With stories whispered, yet untold.
In the calm of dreamer's keep,
Awake the heart, while others sleep.

Dreams Unfolding in Dusk

As daylight fades into the gray,
Soft dreams begin to dance and play.
In twilight's arms, the world transforms,
Creating whispers in gentle swarms.

Petals fall like stars at night,
Each one a spark, a little light.
In the hush, where shadows creep,
Awake the dawn from woven sleep.

With every breath, the silence sings,
Of hidden hopes and fragile things.
Dusk unfolds a canvas wide,
For dreams to travel, hearts to guide.

Trails of Stardust

In the cosmos, trails of light,
Guide the wanderers of the night.
Celestial whispers paint the skies,
Where every star a dreamer lies.

With every step, a story told,
Of paths that shimmer, bold and old.
Dust of starlight softly glows,
A map of dreams where longing flows.

Through cosmic veils, the heart must roam,
In search of love, each traveler's home.
With trails of stardust, spirits soar,
In endless wonder, they explore.

Milton Keynes UK
Ingram Content Group UK Ltd.
UKHW021207261024
450281UK00007B/83

9 789916 907948